Body Language

JON STALLWORTHY was educated at Rugby School, in the Royal West African Frontier Force, and at Magdalen College, Oxford, where he won the Newdigate Prize for Poetry. His books include eight collections of poems, two critical studies of Yeats's poetry, *The Penguin Book of Love Poetry*, *The Oxford Book of War Poetry*, editions of Wilfred Owen's *Complete Poems and Fragments*, and *War Poems*, and two biographies: *Wilfred Owen* (which won the Duff Cooper Memorial Prize, the W.H. Smith Literary Award and the E.M. Forster Award), and *Louis MacNeice* (which won the Southern Arts Literary Prize). In 1998 he published *Rounding the Horn: Collected Poems* and *Singing School*, 'the autobiography we would like all poets to write' (*Oxford Today*). He has been a professor of English Literature at Cornell and Oxford universities, and is now a Senior Research Fellow of Wolfson College, Oxford, and a Fellow of the British Academy.

Also by Jon Stallworthy

Poetry
The Astronomy of Love
Out of Bounds
Root and Branch
Positives
Hand in Hand
The Apple Barrel
A Familiar Tree
The Anzac Sonata: New and Selected Poems
The Guest from the Future
Rounding the Horn: Collected Poems

Anthologies
The Penguin Book of Love Poetry
The Oxford Book of War Poetry
First Lines: Poems Written in Youth, from Herbert to Heaney

Editions
Wilfred Owen: The Complete Poems and Fragments
The Poems of Wilfred Owen
Henry Reed: Collected Poems

Autobiography
Singing School

Biography
Wilfred Owen
Louis MacNeice

Literary criticism
Between the Lines: W.B. Yeats's Poetry in the Making
Vision and Revision in Yeats's Last Poems
Anthem for Doomed Youth: Twelve Soldier Poets of the First World War

Translations
(with Peter France)
Alexander Blok: Selected Poems
Boris Pasternak: Selected Poems

JON STALLWORTHY

Body Language

CARCANET

Acknowledgements

The author wishes to thank those friends who helped, in a variety of ways, with the writing of these poems: Elleke Boehmer, Sandie Byrne, Sarita Cargas, Valentine Cunningham, Julie Curtis, Christine Finn, Alan Gordon, Chris Gosden, Martin Henig, Jenny Houlsby, Simon Keynes, Sue Lloyd, Morag Morris, Sharon Smith, Richard and Kate Sorabji, Roger Tomlin, and Tim Kendall, who published *Skyhorse* as a pamphlet from the Thumbscrew Press in 2002.

Thanks are also due to the editors of *The Independent on Sunday*, *Kunapipi*, *Orbis*, *Oxford Magazine*, *Oxford Poetry*, *Outside Archaeology: Material culture and poetic imagination* (2001), *PN Review*, *Romulus*, *Stand*, *The Dark Horse*, *The Way You Say the World: a celebration for Anne Stevenson* (2003), *The Times* and *The Times Literary Supplement*, in which some of these poems appeared.

'A Word with History' appeared in *Five Centuries of Polish Poetry, 1450–1970*, translated by Jerzy Peterkiewicz, Burns Singer and Jon Stallworthy (2nd edn, 1970).

First published in Great Britain in 2004 by
Carcanet Press Limited
Alliance House
Cross Street
Manchester M2 7AQ

A CIP catalogue record for this book is available from the British Library
ISBN 1 85754 746 2

The publisher acknowledges financial assistance from Arts Council England

Typeset in Bembo by XL Publishing Services, Tiverton
Printed and bound in England by SRP Ltd, Exeter

Contents

Language

Body

Language

In the Beginning

Primal silence, darkness more profound
than any darkness, any silence since,
gave way to the Word of God once
and for always: call it the sound
of ***Light***, a coinage minting the sun,
minting the moon and stars; the sound of ***Land***
dividing the waters cupped in his hand;
Earth blanketing the seeds his ***Seeds*** summon
to furnish the garden where a man would
look at a woman looking at him.

And God looked down on his poem
and saw that it was good.

The sound of ***Man*** breathed life into the earth,
which coalesced and stood erect and gazed
at what the Garden Master's Word had raised
from clay: emerging from the undergrowth,
a moon-white creature woke
the man's still sleeping heart. It stirred,
and set his tongue to groping for the Word
the Garden Master spoke,
creating what came nearer as its name
receded from the listener and
was lost. The nameless nudged his hand.
'Horse,' he said, 'horse.' But it was not the same.

And later, when the Garden Master spoke
of Knowledge, did the horse hear and obey,
eyeing the apple and turning away
as the Woman put out her hand and broke
the primal prohibition? So would we
be happier today
if she had turned away
and left the apple trembling on the tree?

Looking at you – in your linen dress –
looking at me, I wonder: would
we think God's poem good
had we not known his word for nakedness?

Skyhorse

And I looked, and behold a pale horse:
and his name that sat on him was Death.
Revelation 6:8

It is a peculiarity of the Germans to seek omens and warnings from horses. They are kept at public expense in the same groves and woods, white and untouched by any human labour; after they have been harnessed to the sacred chariot, the priest and the king or chieftain of the tribe accompany them and take note of their neighs and snortings. No portent is more trusted, not only by the common people, but by the aristocracy and the priests; for they consider themselves to be the gods' servants, but the horses actually their confidants.

Tacitus: *Germania*, 10, 3–5

Before the gods that made the gods
Had seen their sunrise pass,
The White Horse of the White Horse Vale
Was cut out of the grass.
G.K. Chesterton: *The Ballad of the White Horse*

...that high horse riderless,
Though mounted in that saddle Homer rode...
W.B. Yeats: 'Coole Park and Ballylee, 1931'

The year of the horse

began auspiciously:
the whitest stallion
in the Sacred Grove
mounting the whitest mare.

When prophecies followed,
the praise-singer offered
a millennial ode
to the whitest mare.

1

The first priest of the White Horse tells his son of his commission, *c.*1000 BC

When the skyhorse jumped out of the sky
when his eye
when his breath
when his teeth
death.

Firebreath then
but no firelight
and women talking.
   – Three days dead
but no deathsmell.
   – Whose death, woman? I said.
Their answer only the sound
as of does in flight
of feet shaking the ground.
Four feet, then many,
and voices I knew well
came near and spoke my name.
   – We saw the skyhorse claim him
with his hooves, his teeth,
and yet he moves.
   – And speaks. What cave
darkens your face?
   – No cave, brother. This is the hill
where you and the skyhorse met,
where he gave us fire,
where he set the mark
of his hoof on your head,
making your eyes dark,
ash-white your hair.

Oh then I heard a voice
I knew and did not know
as mine cry
                    Skyhorse,
stargrazer, firebringer,
if you require my eyes
in tribute, gladly
I give them. I will be
your praisesinger.
But if, bestowing light

and dark, you light my eyes
as you have lighted fire,
I and my sons will whiten
the hill's head with your mark,
shadowing your shadow
for all the tribes to praise.

And when the day's eye opened,
mine could see it shine.

2

Priest and poet,
*c.*970 BC

The skyhorse calls
for his bondman,
his priest, who lies
in his shadow
and will not rise
until we let
his spirit go.

The trees add their
lament to ours.
He was their friend,
singing their praise.
In tribute now
his trees let fall
a branch, a bough.

So we must go
and gather them,
men shouldering
the gifts of oak
and ash, children
a holly branch
or mistletoe.

And as we build
the horseman's pyre
see the pictures
I shall sing. –
The horse stamping
his hill, bringing
his people fire.

The horse darkens
a man with light,
a praisesinger
he makes his own.
The man shaping
what his eyes saw.
Flint scraping bone.

The skyhorse leaps
from a white bone
to a burnt hill.
His horseman sows
it with white stones.
On the burnt earth
a starhorse glows.

Skinning the hill
between the stones,
the praisesinger
honours the horse
that honours us,
our guardian
and firebringer.

Bring me a seed
of fire to sow.
It will take root
and its flowers tell
whose spirit goes
to the great cave.
Father, go well.

3

Poet of the shield-wall, AD 871

… a boy on a brown horse
came to the King's tent, and Ethelred called
for Alfred, his brother, and all the thanes.
While the King was in council, word went out
that his cook had seen a silver penny
the boy had been given for bringing news
of Danes on the Ridgeway. King Ethelred,
after the earls had spoken, said: 'We are all
of one mind. We march at cockcrow
and the Lord of Hosts shall lead us.
Tonight, let the armourer look to his anvil,
put sword to whetstone, rivet the shield.'

Firelight set the farm cocks crowing
when the sun still slept under the hill,
nor had it shaken the stars from its hair
until we were mustered and on the march.
The Prince rode ahead of us. His horse
was a white candle in the dark wood.
Then the laggard sun rose, drying the dew
on weapons that soon would again be wet.
On Ashdown, a shield and another shield
flashed not far from the crest. Prince Alfred
turned in his saddle and shouted:
'Shall the heathen stand between this white horse
and his ancient sire?' The army's answer,
hurled round the hills, reached the Danes
as thunder.

They were drawn up
in two divisions. 'Let us do likewise',
the earls said, 'when King Ethelred comes.'
'The Danes do not know he comes. Divide
and strike now,' the Prince replied. Two shield-walls
he ordered, setting old soldiers
among the young. When all were in place,
'Poet,' he said, 'as we step forward,
sing us the lay of the fight at Aclea.'
So I gave them the lay as the green gap
narrowed and the first spears flew.
Eadric, my shire-fellow, dropped at my side.

When the shield-walls clashed, the Prince's sword
was the first to bite. Like a wild boar
he gored earl Sidroc. That was the old earl,
whose son advancing to avenge his sire
bowed his horned helmet. Blood blinded him.
Nor did our earls wield their weapons less fiercely.
Godwin cut down three Danes with gold torques
before he was felled by an evil axe.
With him his brother's son, Wulfstan, fell.
A hard hill we climbed but Heaven's King,
to whom be praise, heard his champion's prayer
at mass that morning. When Ethelred's men
came to the war-play, they came without warning.
Viking eyes were elsewhere as their enemy
struck. We heard then a stallion
utter its war-cry. 'Hear the White Horse,'
earl Aelfwine shouted, and all at once
the heathen broke ranks and ran …

4

Wandering Scholar,
13th century

May morning and a marvel
I climbed a hill to see,
when hedge choirs were singing
of love, but not to me.

The marvel, a white stallion,
where choirs of cherubim
or skylarks were singing
of love, but not to him.

I grieved that his creator
did not take from him there
a rib, when he was sleeping,
to make him a white mare,

as my creator made me –
O Christe, ubi sunt
that hand and fragrant breast,
that mouth and flagrant cunt?

Another man that morning
could answer, but not I
alone on White Horse hill
under a singing sky,

thanking my creator
for hedge choirs, lark and linnet,
for making a green world
with such white marvels in it.

5

Antiquary,
18th century

Gentleman-Commoner, drawn by the lure
Of paquet-boat, post-chaise, and the Grand Tour,
Let Tully be your tutor. 'Call complete
No scholar's learning that is not replete
With knowledge of his native land.' You seek
Antiquities. Must they be marble, Greek
Or Roman? Grander monuments of stone
Await you in a landscape of your own.
See Hadrian's Wall before you seek his Tomb.
His works should be your study, not his doom:
Imperial verses that outlast the bronze
Testudo, eagles and centurions.
Archon of Athens, he was Homer's slave:
An oarsman furrowing the wine-dark wave,
A charioteer, Achilles in the field
Astride a Trojan dazzled by his shield.
He saw with Homer's eyes, but not his own,
The walls of Ilium. We could have shown
Him ramparts overlooking Uffington
As old as those and closer to the sun,
A windy castle that his legions held
Against our fathers, where our fathers felled
The Danish King. The White Horse that red day
Trampled his Raven, and the Norsemen lay
In broken ranks, a banquet for the crows.
Beyond the castle gate, the hillside shows
A people's tribute to a warrior prince,
A White Horse groomed and venerated since.
A nobler horse than Homer's timber mare,
A nobler shade than Hector, unsung, there
Await their chronicler and celebrant.
Look not to Italy or the Levant.
Let your Parnassus be our White Horse hill.
Your muses comb their hair by Letcombe Mill.

6

Rifleman (discharged)
52nd Regiment,
18 June 1832

Whur else ud I be on this uv all days
But yer, givin' God an' 'is 'oss-ship thanks
Fer seventeen yurs an' a sweeter smoke
Than singed me gizzard in the soddin' ranks

Uv riflemen an' barley? 'On thee feeyut!'
The Colonel said, 'An' let they chassers choke
On a Baker's dozen!' 'Alf a dozen an'
They staggert, two more an' they broke.

Out uv the column, over they swothes,
A riderless white 'oss gallopt away.
Boney's pony, us said, leadin' our charge!
God, 'oss, an' baggonet wun us the day.

Not Boney's 'oss, but one sin in a dream
That night. One at 'oose feeyut I ust to play.
One at 'oose feeyut I smokes a pipe
Wi' ole ghosts ev'ry yur on this day.

7

Mother, 1899

Was it for this we climbed the hill,
You with your hurt pride, I with my shame –
A well-scoured wedding ring and still
No child to bear your name?

Was it for this the aching heart,
The prayers, the potions, the remorse,
And you playing the stallion's part
That night under the White Horse?

For this, the anxious hope, the pains,
The truants all day out on the hill
Fighting battles, Saxons and Danes,
The king on his horse – our Will?

Would we have climbed there had we known
What the Colonel's letter would say?
... At Elandslaagte ... your son...
Under his gallant grey...

8

Midsummer Day, 1905

Colonel and others, 1905

1000 hrs. Bandsmen arrive
For practice at the White Horse Inn.
1200 hrs. Bandsmen depart
For Castle in Bandmaster's cart.

Under the eye of the sovereign
Sun, the White Horse Regulars stand
Waving a hat, waving a hand
At the Kingston Lisle United
        (the White Horse Inn's) Brass Band.

1300 hrs. Refreshment
To be taken in Bandsmen's tent.
1330 hrs. Review
By Colonel Hippisley
                                there
Fulfilling at the Midsummer Fair
A major's dream in the Karroo
Of J.P. Sousa, Gilbert and
Sullivan ... played in a green land
By the Kingston Lisle United
        (Hippisley's Own) Brass Band.

Farmers in uniform, we set
Our lips to mouthpieces once wet
In Africa (and when the war
Was over, the band disbanded,
Sold to our Colonel for

A song). Can the Roman dead
Hear us today, as we stand
Our ground on the ramparts they manned
Before the Kingston Lisle United
        (Berkshire's Best) Brass Band?

The Colonel's pride and his despair –
His band performing at the Fair
Buttercup in buttonhole
And no more sense of decent style
Than milkmaids round a maypole.

But
When Uffington and Kingston Lisle
Tug-of-war teams meet hand to hand,
The crowd's pulse is the pulse of the band,
The Kingston Lisle United
(Morrell & Sons') Brass Band.

After the wrestling and the last race,
'Stripping the Willow' takes the place
Of 'British Grenadiers', a rasped
Match reddens a bonfire. Through
Its sparks, they circle two by two,
The strangers and the sweethearts, clasped
Or very shyly hand in hand,
Be-Sousa'd and be-Sullivanned
By the Kingston Lisle United
(Midsummer Night's) Brass Band.

… 11, 12 … the church clocks chime
Across the valley. Fanfare time
For Fortune's waggon-wheel, old wood
Sheathed in new straw, blazing downhill
In pursuit of the sun. How will
It come to rest? Foretelling good
Or ill? And what has Fortune planned
For us – who can scarcely stand –
The Kingston Lisle United
(Hip, hip, Hippisley's Own) Brass Band?

They say the White Horse knows, and neighs
For good luck, snorts for bad. We may's
Well ask. A fortune for a tune,
Played just for him, played in his ear.
Lie back and read the stars…
You hear
A sound? No? Must have dropped off. Soon
Be dawn. United we shall stand –
If sometimes with a helping hand –
The Kingston Lisle United
(The White Horse Vale's) Brass Band.

9

Homeguard, 1940

Ironic really, that men should have scoured
The horse – men with our names – since it was scored
Above Uffington, only for our spades
To bury it: a king's emblem raised
To comfort his folk, discomfort his foes,
Lowered into one of the down's long barrows
Lest the *Luftwaffe* set a course
For Birmingham by the lie of our horse.

No eye in England has seen so much:
Men in skins, men in helmets, the slow march
Of stars across the millennia,
A new star in the east, and many
A falling star – none, I dare say, as bright
As the Messerschmitt that came down last night,
Comet-tail scorching the tree tops, to land
Where legend says the Danes made their last stand.

Did a wind like this that ruffles your mane
Bring you the taunts of axemen and swordsmen
As it did the death-rattle of the plane?
Only ash and an iron cross remain
Of the pilot. We'll put him to bed
When we've billeted you with the older dead.
There'll be many more like that poor Kraut,
And when we've dug them in, we'll dig you out.

10

Ex-homeguard, 1946

'You dug him in,' they said, 'you dig him out.
You know where he is.' That hurt, but they
Couldn't have known and I couldn't explain.
And if I had known what I know today,
I wouldn't have said, standing here in the rain,
'There'll be many more like that poor Kraut.'

The spade that buried him can't resurrect
A German airman known unto God,
But since our Dresden news came through
I've given his grave a flower or two,
Hoping some German might not neglect
An English airman known unto God.

11

Wandering
Scholar,
1999/2000

Setting foot on the hill, on living grass sprung
from grasses trodden by how many feet
grassed over since the horse was young,
I followed again the glimmering line
of a *calligramme* inscribed in chalk
through the last dark of '99.

I thought I should see from the horse's eye
a blazing constellation at my feet,
the valley mirroring the sky,
but the bonfire-makers were all at home,
watching the little people at their games
under a magic mushroom dome.

Would there be bells? Woolstone church held its
tongue.
Midnight was zero hour. The Ridgeway air
shuddered under buffeting
flashes and crashes. Star-shells. Very lights.
I might have been dug in on Vimy Ridge
or bunkered on the Golan Heights.

I lay down by the horse to watch the show,
masque of a murderous century,
but a mist rolled up from below,
rolled up and over me. 'Call me Ishmael',
witness to the tremor, the rumbling sound,
the breaching not of a whale

but a white horse. Lifting its lucent head
it turned a terrible eye to mine,
and a voice at my ear said
'The skyhorse calls for his bondman, his priest.'
So I straddled its back, took hold of its mane,
as the marvellous beast

rose to its feet and through the clouds. Ahead
of us, Black Mountains … Irish Sea … The wind
was stitched with voices, one that said:
'Look at the stars! Look, look up at the skies!
O look at all the fire-folk sitting in the air!'
One whispering: 'Cast a cold eye

On life, on death. Horseman, pass by!'
                                                  We passed
at such a pace – the great stride scissoring
the fabric of the dark so fast –
and such a height that the Atlantic shrank
to a water-jump for a white horse.
And I heard from the further bank,

above the static and the storms, the trace
of other voices, one a woman's,
on the obsidian disc of space:
'I, like the Earth this season, mourn in black,
My Sun is gone so far in's zodiac.'
And I said to myself, we *chase*

the sun – over this sunless continent,
these growling glaciers, voiceless snows, a grey
then a celadon sea. Fast as the sun went,
the horse went faster, from Arctic night
to Burmese afternoon, the Arakan
seen as from a satellite.

There, miles above the mountain tops
I heard a young man say:
'Across scorched hills and trampled crops
The soldiers straggle by.
History staggers in their wake.
The peasants watch them die.'

India was a green leaf on a blue sea ...
Arabia the jawbone of a lion ...
that puckered scar, Gallipoli,
haunted with voices. One I knew:
'Farmers in uniform – much frayed –
here at Cape Helles we parade

without our instruments.'
                                        They never heard
what I would hear above the isles of Greece,
a distant, whispered,
'Seek out – less often sought than found –
a soldier's grave.' 'We didn't have to seek,'
said someone from a killing-ground

closer to home. 'I am the enemy
you killed, my friend ...' 'At Dunkirk I
rolled in the shallows, and the living trod
across me for a bridge ...'
White cliffs we crossed
in the wake of the sun then waking larks
along the Downs' familiar crest.

And there I heard a voice
I knew and did not know
as mine singing below:
'*O Christe, ubi sunt*
that hand and fragrant breast,
that mouth and flagrant cunt?

Another man that morning
could answer, but not I
alone on White Horse hill
under a singing sky.'
And so it was. I found
myself – as the horse went to ground –

on my back in long grass, surrounded
by voices interwoven with the wind:
that of a horseman who founded
a tribe singing a lay that extolled
the horse, as I walked down to Uffington
and into a future not foretold.

Dreamhorse

Laddie, we called him, Laddie the horse
our father rescued from a house
the auctioneer was knocking down,
knocking down, knocking down,
his little hammer knocking down,
carriage clock and rocking horse.

Conceived in a horse-drawn century,
a foal delivered by carpentry
from the dark of a sapwood womb
to paint-shop and tack-room,
for children to canter and groom
in a mechanised century.

The girls' Black Beauty, my Bucephalus,
my Copenhagen, Pegasus –
responding to the spur
that drove him over
battlefield and frontier –
grew old along with us.

His mane receded. Cowboy spurs cut up
his flanks. He lost a stirrup,
but horse-doctors today
can keep old age at bay –
in rocking horses, anyway.
Grandson, let me give you a leg up.

Body

Before Setting Out

Before setting out on a journey,
the Russians sit down with a glass
of champagne (if they have it) or *kvass*
and take stock of whatever they see
themselves taking or leaving
for others to take or leave,
the luggage of love and grief
'not wanted on voyage'.

                                        An evening,
a garden I think of as mine
(and others have thought of as theirs),
a couple of garden chairs
and, yes, a bottle of wine
to lubricate memory, bring
to this slanting light what has been lost
and found: love first and last,
a splinter of the true sun colouring
the colourless. Eyes return
to spring in a wilderness, once
a garden and a garden since;
a spring in which to learn
the names of apple trees and where
the snowdrop hides that will be found
when children start clearing the ground.
Bonfire smoke sweetens the air.
If only I could learn
from the Russet to let my leaves go
downwind to the bonfire, and so
sweeten the village as others burn
bitterly. We are at war
again, but laughter can be heard
above the axe in the orchard,
wheels slowing at the door.

A Ferry for Bishop Jim

died at sea, 19 September 2003

Frater Ave atque Vale
Catullus and Tennyson

A white cliff with a thousand eyes
saluted the returning sun,
a white ship with a thousand eyes,
all of them open but one.

A man whose heart held multitudes,
the statesmen's counsellor, champion
of the stateless, in the night
had slipped his moorings and moved on,

as the ferries we watched today,
big blue and white Aegean ones,
leaving the harbour's arms were lost
to sight, our sight, but not the sun's.

Tinos, Greece, September 2003

The White Cloud

Just us, again together, and
an old friend for your voyage – Beethoven.
(If you can hear me, squeeze my hand.)

The ferry is already manned,
but till you're called aboard, let's listen
to Beethoven together, and

perhaps begin to understand
things sons and fathers leave unspoken.
(If you can hear me, squeeze my hand.)

Do you remember our weekend
in wartime, haymaking while the sun shone?
Our pitchforks toss and gather, and

a white cloud shadowing the land
travels ahead of us on our wagon.
(If you can hear me, squeeze my hand.)

The *Pastoral* advances, grand
as the great cloud, as I would have it when
again we are together (and
if you can hear me, squeeze my hand).

Handiwork

We knew he was dying,
my father, but his hands
didn't know. Still plying
their trade in his last sleep,
they were stitching the lip
of a wound only he
in his dream could see.

Will *my* hands be as true,
to *their* trade? I would wish
myself a dream that you
would guess, if you could see
these fingers on their sheet
tenderly beating time,
making our bodies rhyme.

The Motor Vessel Anichka

The Sligo Champion tells me that down on Sligo quay,
where three years ago she took shelter from a gale,
the *Anichka* (then *St Peter*, formerly
Shevchenko) is up for sale.

I will go down and buy her, and buy her for a song,
with her two blue funnels and her three steel decks
fourteen metres at the waist, ninety-five metres long.
How could the Russians mistake her sex?

I will go down and buy her if you will be my crew
and share the captain's cabin in the warm white nights,
as we sail her home together in shirt-sleeve weather, you
and me, under the Northern Lights.

And we will have some music if you will be my crew:
accordions awash with the river songs of Russia, gull
and wind and bow-wave, and the song of ourselves, you
and me, under the sign of Chagall.

Le Violon d'Ingres

Man Ray, inventive fellow,
seeing the girl who sat
for him hipped like a cello,
portrayed her as that.

And did they then make music –
as we would, I know,
if you would be my cello
and I could be your bow?

A Foreign Tongue

It dawned on me this was no common dream
of a dark truth translated into light
but, rather, a translation more extreme
into a foreign tongue – foreign that night
until I tasted what the eyes said, heard
hands that were strangers talk as twins with no
word spoken. Incandescent, the word
was flesh, no longer the shadow
of what it signified.

                                        And, yes, I woke
into a world of shadows, a world where
we used to hear of presences who spoke
a foreign tongue that, one day, we might share.
I half believed it true, but now I know
that somehow, somewhere, sometime it is so.

Lioness

The Serengeti lioness
arches her back, retracts her claws
to cuff a boisterous cub,
and licks her travelled paws.
She is at home in her body
as you are at home in yours.

The lion that, shamming sleep,
was watching her strolls through
a bevy of princesses
to share her shade. As you
are at home in your body,
I am at home there too.

Taking Breath

'You take my breath away.'
'As you take mine,' I said
as truthfully, the day
we christened the new bed.

The breath I borrowed there
I give you back in this,
mixed with my own, a fair
exchange, an equal kiss.

Libation

A half-empty bottle
with a Château label
was dancing with two glasses
on a bedside table,

two glasses of Chablis
tangoing cheek to cheek,
making as they crossed the floor
eine kleine Nachtmusik,

dancing till they dropped
and dropping poured a rich
libation to the god
or to the goddess. Which?

Hers

Greek sponge, speak to me
of bounty under water,
not only under sea.

Speak also to her –
with all your succulent mouths
speak of another.

Clasp

When will it be, and where,
that my ambassador
loosens the sheaf of your hair
as many times before

but then for the last time?
My clasp unclasped. Will you
remember then what I'm
remembering – a new

lover, my left hand
under your head, your hair
snared in my fingers, and
my writing hand elsewhere?

What's in a Name?

One of the sounds of heaven, if
it's yours she whispers like a spell,
whispers, and then cries out. But if,
in some cruel dream, you hear the same
voice crying another name –
one of the sounds of hell.

Exorcism

Whenever the child cried out at night,
he would be rescued by a blade of light,
a mother's paper and pencil. 'Draw
me the horror you say you saw,
and your drawing will drive it away.'

Dear exorcist, again today
your grown child seemed to hear you say
'Write it down and drive it away.'

I was trying to escape, cutting a path
uphill in the sulphurous aftermath
of some Armageddon, sensed but not seen
in the valley where we had been.
No sound but the bark of a dog, somewhere
ahead or behind us, rasping the air
as we with our gasping, she and I.
Her voice then behind me: 'Look how the sky
lightens along the ridge. If we can keep
heading for that, who knows, we could sleep
in a happy valley.'
                                        It was true –
the bright ridge a blade to the rescue.
I turned to take her hand, but as I did
her body, like a candle, melted
into smoke, a writhing ghost the wind
snatched from my arms.

                                        Real or imagined
the animal cry that woke me? Hers
or mine? No exorcist answers
as I write this, and an Arctic light
uncovers the bedspread and the white
pillow warmed, through other nights, by one
whose smile was my sunrise. My un-
returning, subterranean sun.

Hunting the Lark

for Tony Hecht

‘A poet who’s never heard
the hundred-foot-high cascade
of Shakespeare’s and Shelley’s bird!’
Remember, I made you wade –

you in your city shoes –
across a prosaic field
(O for an urban muse,
I guess you were thinking – yes?)

until, with perfect timing,
a small bird climbing
a precipitous cloud
set earth and sky rhyming.

I haven’t heard the lark
for two years now.
It doesn’t sing in the dark,
but today, remembering how

Shelley’s bird sang for us
once when the sun still
would lift itself off its arse
without a white pill,

today, your birthday, I hear
that rhyming cascade again
as a farmer on parched earth
hears – can you hear it? – rain.

Osip Mandelstam Proposes a Toast

I drink to Hussars' epaulettes, and to all the charges against me:
to asktrakhan coats, and to asthma, to St Petersburg ennui,
to the music of Savoyard pines, and the fumes of the Champs-
Elysées,
to Parisian oils, and to roses on the seat of a Rolls coupé.
I drink to a jug of Swiss cream, and to Biscay's sparkling wave,
to the hauteur of red-headed memsahibs, and quinine from the
White Man's Grave.
I drink, but have not yet decided for which I should clap
my hands: ebullient Asti Spumante or Châteauneuf du Pape …

Translated from the Russian of Osip Mandelstam

A Word with History

Old Mother History, Queen of Them All,
how you enjoy raising a stink!
Orion peeps through the bars in the wall
and here we sit, you and me, in clink.

You're giving me the same old patter-song
with the same half-derisive leer.
So side by side we go clanking along,
you since Time was, I since last year.

Immortal madam, why and whence
the passion for paradox you display?
Do you really think that it makes sense
to poison the world's blood in this way?

For in the whole wide world I see
nothing but war, conflict and crisis.
Hardly the time, would you agree,
for us to be doing time like this?

Why should a revolutionary poet
rot to death in this Soviet hole?
Dear History, it strikes a jarring note.
Surely one of us is playing the fool?

Shame on you, madam, Queen of Them All;
let me out of Zamarstynov then.
(And on the other side of the wall
we'll soon be sent down again.)

Translated from the Polish of Władsław Broniewski

A Round

Lead ore lifted from a Cornish mine,
married in a furnace to Cornish tin,
their one flesh pewter, a barnacled plate
salvaged from the ribs of a ship of the line,
in Cape Town market sold for a florin,
bartered for biltong in the Free State,
a farmer's wedding present for his bride
to shine, until – with the waggon-team
taken, the farm in flames – she cried
as he melted it down, tilting its gleam
to the lips of his bullet-mould, one
of whose slugs would open a seam
in a Cornish miner's son.

Edward Thomas's Fob Watch

Face to face, hand in hand,
never a day apart
until the last day and
the wordless heart to heart.

In the House of the Poet

I am the twisted man
whose head your hammer tapped
breaking the pumice skin,
letting the dark out,
letting the light in.

Dark of my marriage-day,
known to the calendar
as the Day of the Dead.
When Hades' gates open
Pompeii shakes, we said.

It had shaken for days –
at nights, shaking the bed
soon to be garlanded.
I took this to be
propitious augury,

until from the mountain,
as from a hive, I saw
the shades break free. They came
swarm after stinging swarm,
clouds interspersed with flame,

tormenting land and sea
with their own torment. Then,
letting their torches fall,
the legions of the dead
made ghosts of us all,

the husband and the wife
sealed in separate tombs,
and all those poems lost
but one (the last) in mis-
translation: this.

Notes

p. 11 'Skyhorse'. 'None of the chalk figures of England has excited so much interest as the mysterious, dragon-like creature sprawling along the edge of the downs at Uffington. So different from all the other white horses and so obviously very much older than they are, it seems to present a challenge and demand an explanation. Who made it? When? Why?'

Archaeologists have now answered the second of these questions asked by Morris Marples (in his book *White Horses and Other Hill Figures*, 1949, p. 28). Optically stimulated luminescence dating of samples from the White Horse's V-shaped chalk-filled trench show it to have been cut approximately 3,000 years ago. Poems 1 and 2 offer hypothetical answers to Marple's first and third questions.

p. 17 The most detailed account of the battle of Ashdown in AD 871 is that of the monk Asser. See *Alfred the Great: Asser's Life of King Alfred and other contemporary sources*, translated with an Introduction and Notes by Simon Keynes and Michael Lapidge, 1983.

Aclea. In AD 851, King Aethelwulf and an army drawn from all over Wessex defeated a large Danish force at Aclea (a site now identified with Ockley in Surrey).

p. 19 *Wandering Scholar.* The classic account of the medieval *Vagantes*, their Latin 'lovesongs and springsongs' is Helen Waddell, *The Wandering Scholars*, 7th ed. (revised), 1934.

p. 20 *Tully.* Marcus Tullius, 106–43 BC, Roman senator, better known as Cicero.

Hadrian. Publius Aelius Hadrianus, AD 76–138, was elected archon of Athens in AD 111 or 112 and, as poet and soldier, may be presumed an admirer of Homer. He visited Britain in AD 121 or 122, when Emperor of Rome, and ordered the building of what came to be known as Hadrian's Wall. He was buried in the mausoleum he had built in Rome.

A windy castle. The ancient camp, known as Uffington Castle, on the west of the downs above the White Horse.

p. 21 On 18 June 1815, at the Battle of Waterloo, the Light Brigade, of which the 52nd Regiment formed a part, drove Napoleon's Chasseurs across a cornfield in a violent attacking manoevre. See

Elizabeth Longford: *Wellington: The Years of the Sword*, pp. 477–8 for a full account of the battle.

'oss. Horse.

feeyut. Feet.

chassers. Chasseurs.

Baker's Dozen. The men of the 52nd Regiment, the Oxfordshire Light Infantry, were armed with Baker rifles.

swothes. Swathes.

Boney's Pony. At Waterloo, Napoleon was riding his white charger.

p. 22 *Elandslaagte*. On one of the few occasions when British cavalry were committed in the Anglo-Boer War, a squadron each of the 5th Lancers and the 5th Dragoon guards charged a Boer stronghold at Elandslaagte ('Elands Leap'), Natal, on 21 October 1899, killing or wounding most of its defenders.

p. 23 *Colonel Hippisley*. William Henry Hippisley, 1855–1908, served in the Zulu Campaign of the South African War. Retiring to the village of Sparsholt at the foot of White Horse Hill, he kitted out the Kingston Lisle United Brass Band at his own expense.

p. 24 *Morrell & Sons*. Oxfordshire brewers since 1782.

a bonfire. A reference to the Midsummer Eve bonfires around which young villagers would dance, leaping across them for good luck. A burning cartwheel would be rolled from a hilltop and, 'if it reached the valley still burning, to be quenched in river or pond', it was thought that 'Destiny would smile'. (Laurence Whistler, *The English Festivals*, 1947, pp. 166–7.)

p. 25 In 1940, the White Horse, a familiar landmark to German bombers, was turfed over.

p. 27 *calligramme*. Guillaume Apollinaire, 1880–1918, called his 'shaped poems' *calligrammes*.

'Call me Ishmael'. The opening sentence of Herman Melville's *Moby Dick*.

'Look at the stars!' G.M. Hopkins, 'The Starlight Night', lines 1–2.

p. 28 '*Cast a cold eye*', W.B. Yeats, 'Under Ben Bulben', lines 92–4.

'*I, like the Earth this season*'. Anne Bradstreet, 'A Letter to Her

Husband, Absent upon Public Employment', lines 7–8.

'*Across scorched hills*'. Alun Lewis, 'The Peasants', lines 9–12.

'*Seek out*'. Lord Byron, 'On This Day I Complete my Thirty-Sixth Year', lines 37–8.

p. 29 '*I am the enemy*'. Wilfred Owen, 'Strange Meeting', line 70.

'*At Dunkirk*'. Sidney Keyes, 'The Foreign Gate', lines 218–20.

p. 49 'A Word with History'. (*Rozmowa z Historią*), from the volume *Wiersze*, published posthumously in Paris (1962). Last stanza, line 2: Zamarstinov (*Zamarstyńow*), a suburb in Lvov with a jail, in which Broniewski (1897–1962) was put by the Soviet occupants. The poem has a few slang expressions about 'doing time', such as *na kiblu*, which literally means 'sitting on a prison bucket'.

p. 51 'Edward Thomas's Fob Watch'. Stopped by the blast of the German shell that killed him at 7.36 a.m. on 9 April, Easter Monday, 1917.